The Carnivore Diet

Delicious recipes meat based

Author

Maria D. Harley

What is the Carnivore Diet, and how does it work?

We always seem to hear about a new diet plan that has been released. Each one will have its own set of rules and foods that you are permitted to consume, and they all appear to be quite different. The Mediterranean diet emphasizes the consumption of a variety of healthy carbohydrates, grains, and vegetables. The vegetarian diet emphasizes the consumption of whole grains and fruits and vegetables rather than meat products. Then there's the ketogenic diet, which eliminates carbohydrates in favor of a high-fat diet. And there's the Paleo diet, which encourages you to eat only the foods that your forefathers could get their hands on. These are just a few of the various diet plans available, and while each one promises to provide you with some of the weight loss and other benefits that you seek, it is time to learn more about the carnivore diet and what it entails.

The carnivore diet is a brand-new way of eating that claims to help you lose weight and feel better in no time. This diet requires you to consume no carbohydrates, as well as no fruits or vegetables. In fact, you'll have to limit yourself to only eating meat. But, before your inner burger aficionado jumps for joy, it's important to hear some of the diet plan's specifics.

The carnivore diet, also known as the all-meat diet, consists of eating almost nothing but meat for every meal, all of the time. This means you'll be eating a lot of protein, a lot of fat, and almost no carbohydrates.

Some nutritional conventional wisdom will be challenged by this. This means you'll disregard the advice to eat plenty of grains, fiber, and vegetables in order to stay healthy. Many popular diet plans, such as the vegetarian and vegan diets, include this advice. Because this diet plan will spend so much time focusing on meats and proteins, with no other options from produce or carbs, you might expect it to cause weight gain, digestive issues, and high cholesterol levels, to name a few of the health issues.

This diet plan, on the other hand, proves that conventional wisdom, especially when it comes to health and nutrition, isn't always correct. The carnivore diet is based on the idea that our forefathers were able to eat mostly meat because gathering a lot of fruits and vegetables was inefficient in terms of energy expenditure. According to this theory, our bodies have evolved to run at their best and most efficient levels on a diet centered on meats.

When comparing the carnivore diet to the vegan diet, according to George Ede MD, there is a historical observation that we can look at. This theory will help you understand why the carnivore diet works so well and why you should consider using it to achieve your weight loss goals. The following historical observation from George Ede MD supports the theory that the carnivore diet:

"To the best of my knowledge, the world has yet to produce a civilization that has eaten a vegan diet from birth to death, whereas there are numerous examples throughout recorded history of people from a variety of cultural, ethnic, and geographical backgrounds who have lived on predominantly meat diets for decades, lifetimes, and generations."

It can be difficult to understand how the carnivore diet can be beneficial to your health, especially after hearing so much about how healthy carbs and produce are. Not only does it not harm the body, but if done correctly, it can actually improve your health.

This method, however, may not be suitable for everyone. Children, for example, should not follow this type of diet because it is critical that they obtain the nutrients they require from other sources. This diet is best avoided by pregnant and breastfeeding women, as well as others who need to monitor their diet with the help of a medical professional. The carnivore diet, on the other hand, can help most healthy adults lose weight and improve their health while eating foods that are good for them.

What is the Carnivore Diet, and how does it work?

Now that we've looked at the carnivore diet and what it entails, it's time to look at what foods you can eat, what foods you should avoid, and more.

The principles of the carnivore diet are straightforward. This is a good thing because many people struggle to stick to a diet plan that has so many rules and requirements that they can't remember them. This diet plan's simplicity can make it much easier to stick to.

There are four main types of foods that you can eat if you follow the carnivore diet. You can eat meat, cheese, butter, and eggs, for the most part. You can also consume a few of the zero-calorie foods available, such as spices and coffee. Many people use Bulletproof coffee to boost their energy levels in the morning, so MCT oil can be included in this diet plan as well.

As you can see, the foods listed above are high in protein and fat, but they have almost no carbs. And, like some of the other diet plans out there, such as the Paleo diet, nuts and vegetables, as well as fruits, must be avoided because they contain too many carbs and were not part of the diet of those on whom this diet is based.

Carbohydrates must be limited when following the carnivore diet. All of your old favorites will be cut out, including fruits and vegetables, bread, baked goods, and pasta. This is a very low-carb diet. This is such a low number that you should avoid eating any meat or cheese unless it contains a small amount of carb. This can be difficult to adjust to at first, especially if you're used to eating a lot of processed and fast foods, but it can be extremely beneficial to your overall health.

The Most Important Advantages of Following This Diet Plan

When it comes to the carnivore lifestyle, the key advantages are the next thing to consider. This diet plan has a lot of advantages. If you can give up your sweet tooth in exchange for a diet rich in meats and other fatty foods, this diet plan is ideal. This type of diet allows you to eat high-quality meats and steaks every day.

Another advantage of this diet plan is that if you cut out or eliminate all carbs, your body will enter ketosis. Ketosis is a metabolic state in which the body burns stored fat instead of carbohydrates for energy. Weight loss, strength, ADHD management, and other benefits have all been linked to ketosis.

The carnivore lifestyle can help you achieve ketosis. You'll also notice that ketosis happens much faster than on other diets because you can limit your carb intake. Although you may need some time to adjust to the ketogenic diet, it can significantly improve your health and energy levels.

Another advantage of the carnivore diet is that many people realize that moderation is not always the best option. A small amount of sugar, or even a snack, may be too much for you. Although you can control how much sugar you consume, the temptation to consume more is too strong. You will be tempted to eat too much once you have had a taste.

For these individuals, a carnivore diet is a viable option. It does not necessitate a high-sugar or high-carbohydrate diet. These are to be completely eliminated. This is a great way to ensure that you stick to the diet plan and lose the weight you want.

These are just a few of the points to keep in mind. If you were a big fan of sugar and carbs before starting the diet, you'll have a lot of cravings. For the first few weeks, the cravings will be intense. To overcome them, you'll have to put in a lot of effort. Carbs are good for your body. These carbs provide a quick source of energy for your body. Because your body is inefficient at consuming all of the carbohydrates and glucose you eat, these carbs can cause weight gain.

As a result, there is a lot of body fat.

Although the cravings will pass, you must be strong enough to prevent them from returning. As your body adjusts to different foods, this can last anywhere from a week to a couple of weeks. Staying hydrated and eating enough to meet your energy needs will yield results.

When you live a carnivore lifestyle, you will also be able to lose weight. The carnivore lifestyle has proven to be successful for many people. It all depends on the amount of weight you want to lose.

Even those who started the program in good health lost six to eight pounds. If you are obese or overweight, you can lose even more weight.

If you've tried other diets in the past and are looking to lose weight, the carnivore diet is for you. You can lose weight if you can effectively eliminate sugars and carbohydrates. When you stop chasing your cravings for meat, cheese, and butter, you'll notice a significant difference in weight loss and health benefits.

This diet plan is still in its infancy. It is still relatively new, despite the many great benefits and outcomes that have been discovered with it.

You should proceed with caution and pay close attention to how your body responds. Some people will respond positively, while others will find it unsuitable. It may take some trial and error to figure out which one is best for you.

How to Begin Following a Carnivore Diet

Before you begin living the carnivore lifestyle, there are a few things you should know. To begin this type of diet, you must be mentally prepared. This will ensure that you stay healthy and achieve your goals.

If you're thinking about going on a carnivore diet, you should talk to your doctor first. Consult your doctor about the diet and get his or her advice. You should also make sure you don't have any medical issues that could make this diet more difficult or dangerous for you. Consult your doctor about the diet plan to ensure that you are in good health.

While you're at the doctor's office, have your blood tested. This blood test should be done two to three months after you start your diet plan to see how effective it is. Although you may lose weight and gain confidence, the results you achieve in terms of your health can be quite remarkable.

When you begin your carnivore diet, you will notice changes in your energy, weight, digestion, and weight. It's a good idea to keep track of these changes every day, or at least once a week. Even if they follow this diet plan, everyone is different. It can have a significant impact on your ability to stick to the diet plan. You can also make a comparison between how it works and how you felt at the start.

Next, keep in mind that the first two weeks will be the most challenging. Expect changes in your energy, concentration, and appetite. This plan will make you feel great if you can stick with it for the long run. During the first week, you may feel hungry, angry, or irritable.

This is because you're attempting to switch from carbs to fat as a source of energy. It will take some time for you to adjust. If you can, choose a week that isn't too hectic. You might be able to work from home or take a break to deal with your mood swings. Slow down your work schedule so you have more time to sleep in and relax. This will make it easier for you to stick to the diet plan and achieve the results you want.

Experimenting with as many different options as possible may be necessary. You might lose your appetite for meat and other meat-related products. This means you'll have to think outside the box to come up with the right meals for you. It's possible to get sick of steak if you eat too much of it the first week.

This does not imply that you must abandon your diet. All you have to do now is look for other ways to assist you. For example, you may need to increase your intake of butter and cheese, as well as fish and hamburgers. The diet plan emphasizes steak consumption, and you should increase your vegetable intake on a daily basis. If you're looking for a way to break up the monotony or mix things up, this is a great option.

There are a few ways to cheat, and these can help you stick to the diet for the first week. If you cheat, you should not do so. Peanut butter, for example, is permitted under certain conditions. Although it is not as harmful as Twinkies, it can still provide you with the necessary fats and proteins. You'll have to get rid of it, but it could be a great way to assist you.

While you're getting used to your new diet, make adjustments.

Finally, be ready for any appetite fluctuations you may encounter. For a few days, you'll feel fuller, but then you'll be unable to eat anything. There will be days when you are constantly hungry and cannot consume enough food to satisfy your hunger.

Your appetite will begin to level out after a few weeks. It's crucial to play around with portion sizes to find the ones that work best. This allows you to eat enough throughout the day without feeling hungry while also preventing overeating. Until you find that balance, make sure you eat healthy, carnivore-friendly food at all times of the day. This way, your body will be fine if it isn't hungry. You can always grab an extra snack if you get hungry.

What Is the Difference Between a Ketogenic and a Carnivore Diet?

Although the carnivore and ketogenic lifestyles appear to be very similar, there are many differences. To begin, the ketogenic diet necessitates a reduction in carbohydrate consumption. The ketogenic diet, on the other hand, requires you to consume as many green vegetables and fruits as possible. Vegetables are still considered healthy on the ketogenic diet. Green vegetables are high in nutrients and low in carbohydrates, so you should eat them.

Vegetables are not allowed in the carnivore diet. On a carnivore diet, it's not about limiting carbohydrate intake. It's all about avoiding carbs completely. This is not the diet for you.

The macronutrient content of the diets is the second distinction. The macronutrient ratio of the ketogenic diet will be approximately 75 percent fat, 5% carbs, and 20% protein. This is determined by the maximum number of calories you can consume per day. There is no set macronutrient ratio in the carnivore diet. Instead, the follower should prioritize eating fatty meats, and the rest will take care of itself.

When comparing the macronutrients of a typical carnivore's diet to the ketogenic diet, you'll notice that the carnivore's diet has more protein and less fat. However, the carbohydrate intake would be significantly reduced.

The ketogenic diet necessitates a reduction in protein consumption. While you are permitted to consume some, it is critical that you do not consume excessive amounts. Healthy fats, on the other hand, can be obtained from a variety of sources, including dairy products and oils. Cheese and butter are the only dairy products allowed on the carnivore diet. All of the other foods must be high in protein. The fat-to-protein ratios may differ slightly.

The inclusion of dairy products in the carnivore and ketogenic diets is the third thing you might notice. The ketogenic diet forbids the consumption of dairy products and encourages you to avoid any that contain carbohydrates. Milk and dairy products are allowed in the carnivore diet because they are animal products.

This is why, on a carnivore diet, you should eat aged cheese rather than milk. While some of these foods are permissible on a carnivore diet, most people will prefer butter, eggs, and fatty meats, as well as aged cheese.

Frequently Asked Questions about Carnivore Diet

It's natural to have a lot of questions about the carnivore diet. This diet differs significantly from what we've seen in many other diets. You'll almost certainly have a lot of questions. Some of the most important questions to consider when starting a carnivore diet are:

Is it really necessary to eat all vegetables?

Fruits and vegetables are necessary for our overall health. This has been a recurring theme throughout our lives. Vegetables may not be as important as we once thought, according to research. Despite their high vitamin and nutrient content, vegetables may not be as nutritious as other foods.

According to High Steaks, these vegetables and fruits may contain a variety of nutrients, but they may also contain a large number of harmful ones. These anti-nutrients can bind to the same receptors as the good minerals, making it more difficult for the body to absorb them. Some nutrients are lost during the cooking process, while others are used in a way that makes them difficult to absorb or use.

Do I have any digestive problems as a result of my carnivore diet?

Some people worry that if they switch to a carnivore diet, they will have issues with fiber and won't be able to eat enough vegetables. Some people experience minor digestive problems. Many people found that switching to a carnivore diet solved their digestive problems. Even if you eat fewer fiber-rich foods, most people will not experience these digestive issues.

Is it necessary for me to take a fiber supplement while following this diet plan?

If you don't eat a lot of junk food, you won't need to eat as much unhealthy food. On a carnivore diet, this is what will happen naturally. This is an analogy: Tylenol may be beneficial for someone with neck pain, but it is not for someone who does not have neck pain. It could also have unfavorable side effects in people who don't need it.

Is it okay to consume a lot of red meat?

You must consider the numerous other factors that can influence your nutrition and lifestyle. If you eat too much sugar and don't exercise enough, you won't be as healthy. If you avoid sugar and eat healthy foods, red meat isn't harmful.

Is it necessary for me to be concerned about my cholesterol?

There is some debate about whether fat and meat raise cholesterol levels. When it comes to cholesterol and everything else in our bodies, there are numerous variables to consider. If you eat a lot of sugar and fat at the same time, this will be different.

There are numerous studies that demonstrate that fat is not the primary cause of our health problems. Sugar is to blame for these issues. Correlation, on the other hand, does not always imply causation. Another important factor to consider is exercise. Instead of staying indoors and doing nothing, getting some exercise can help lower your cholesterol levels.

When you learn about the carnivore lifestyle, you'll have a lot of questions. This is a nutritious diet that emphasizes the consumption of meat and healthy fats. It also allows you to almost completely eliminate carbs. It is unlikely to alter our understanding of traditional dietary advice.

It will, however, make a significant difference in your health.

On the Carnivore Diet, what foods am I allowed to eat?

We now have a better understanding of the carnivore lifestyle. Let's look at some of the foods you can eat on the diet. Because of all the restrictions, it can be difficult to follow. It's simple to choose because there are only four foods you can eat. The carnivore lifestyle is for those who want fast results without having to adhere to a lot of rules and regulations. Let's take a look at what you can eat and what you should avoid if you're living a carnivore lifestyle.

Foods You Can Consume

The food you eat should be the most important part of your carnivore diet. The majority of your calories will come from fattening meats. This is an excellent choice because it provides you with the healthy fats, protein, and energy you require throughout the day. There's nothing wrong with eating until you're full.

When following this diet plan, you can eat a variety of meats. The following are some of the best beef cuts to focus on (beef is the best meat source when following this diet plan):

1. Animal organs are used. Although it is not required, it can assist you in mixing things up if necessary.

2. Beef, ground

3. Roasts. Brisket, chick, or prime rib are all options.

4. Steaks. Strip, sirloin, and chuckeye steaks are among the many cuts available. A word about organ meats. Some people believe that in order to get enough nutrition, you must eat organ meats. The diet plan does not call for this. Eating these meats has a lot of advantages, and it adds variety and nutrients to your diet. Organ meat, on the other hand, is optional if you don't want to eat it.

On this diet, you don't have to limit your beef intake. Lamb, pork, chicken, and fish are also options.

When it comes to the beverages you want to drink as part of this diet, you have a lot of options. Sodas, alcohol, and other alcoholic beverages are prohibited. These will have added sugars and carbs, which you should avoid if you're following this diet plan.

When following a carnivore diet, water is the most important source of water to consume. You can drink it plain or add mineral or carbonated water to it. Bone broth, tea, and coffee are also options.

You can also get plenty of fatty foods from a variety of other sources. Hard cheeses, heavy whipping cream, butter, and eggs are among them. You can include these in your diet as often as you want. Healthy spices can also be added to the mix. While following this diet plan, you will be able to enjoy a wide variety of meals and combinations.

The Foods to Stay Away From

When following a carnivore diet, there are a number of foods to avoid. When following this diet plan, you should avoid a variety of foods. They could have too many carbohydrates or be incompatible with the foods our forefathers ate.

Even though these foods are common in the American diet, your body may not be able to handle them. The first food group you should eliminate from your diet is carbohydrates.

Carbohydrates are a popular food choice among many people. Carbs are something they enjoy.

For meals, they can eat whole grains, bread, pasta, and cereals. Whole grains, according to conventional nutritional wisdom, are beneficial. They supply the body with beneficial fiber and B-vitamins.

These whole grains will be too high in carbohydrates, and there are other ways to get these nutrients. It's time to deprive them of their carnivore diet. These whole grains should be avoided because they will prevent you from achieving ketosis. Learn about other carnivore options and how to say goodbye to whole grains you've enjoyed in the past.

You should also avoid eating the same fruits and vegetables as you did previously. Fresh produce has many benefits, but you should avoid them if you want to follow this diet. While they are rich in healthy nutrients, fresh produce can also be beneficial for your health. However, there is a lot of antinutrients that can lead to other health problems.

The body may not be able to absorb or consume certain nutrients from the produce it consumes without some fat. You can eat as many fruits and vegetables as you like, but if your body doesn't get enough healthy fats, you will end up wasting all the good nutrients.

You must reduce the amount of fresh vegetables you eat when you follow the carnivore diet. It

might be challenging, particularly if you have been accustomed to consuming enough of nutritional nutrients from fresh fruit in the past. There are other methods to acquire the nutrients you need from vegetables (primarily from the healthier meats you should consume), so you need to remove them as soon as you can.

Also, keep in mind all of the processed foods and baked goods you've grown accustomed to on the traditional American diet. If you enjoy baking and consume a lot of carbs and sugars, this is a difficult diet to follow. Sugar cravings and withdrawals can be difficult to overcome, making it difficult to avoid sugary foods.

There are many healthy and delicious foods you can eat instead of following the diet plan to achieve the same results.

Adjusting to a carnivore lifestyle can take some time. The more unhealthy foods you consumed before beginning the carnivore lifestyle, the more difficult it will be to adjust in the coming weeks.

You'll soon be able to see the benefits once you've gotten used to the new way of eating and learned to overcome sugar cravings, as well as once you've noticed the positive effects of ketosis on your weight and overall health.

So, how about the drinks?

When working with a carnivore diet, you must be cautious about the beverages you consume. Your primary source of hydration will almost certainly be water. If you eat a diet high in animal products, you will feel thirstier than you did previously. To avoid dehydration, keep a bottle of water on hand at all times.

Plain water, mineral water, and carbonated water are all permissible to consume. It's impossible to put too much in the water. To make the water more delicious, you cannot add flavorings, fruits, or vegetables. Drink plain water to keep it simple. You'll get the proper amount of hydration this way.

Some, but not all, carnivore diets allow green tea consumption. Because it is an animal product, some methods will accept milk. Others won't eat it because it's high in carbohydrates.

You must eliminate a variety of beverages from your diet in order to achieve success. Alcohol in any form must be avoided at all costs. Because they are typically made of fruits and grains, they are not suitable for carnivores. You'll have to avoid most fruit juices, milk, and all types of sodas as well.

Are spices available?

On this diet plan, you can eat certain spices. For carnivores, the majority of spices are allowed. They can be used to change the way you eat and add flavor to food. Salt and pepper, two of the most commonly used spices in this type of diet, will be found in almost all of the recipes.

Salt should be used sparingly in certain meals. If you have high blood pressure, limiting your salt consumption is a good idea. Even if high blood pressure is not a concern for you right now, reducing salt intake to avoid high blood pressure is a good idea.

Spices of other kinds should also be considered. Some of these spices can be used to enhance the flavor of your meals without raising your blood pressure.

All condiments should be left out of the dish. Bone broth can be used, and it can also be used as a sauce. Animal products are not used in the production of condiments. They're high in sugars and carbohydrates, and they're unhealthy, so they should be avoided in a carnivore diet.

It's critical that you only consume nutritious foods. Animal products are the only foods you can eat. If you can stick to these foods, you will see incredible health and weight loss results.

What are the advantages of the Carnivore Diet for your health?

If you're looking for a new diet that doesn't require you to consume carbohydrates and is also suitable for people who don't want to consume a lot of fruits and vegetables, the carnivore diet is the best option. As your primary source of fuel, this diet plan will emphasize fatty meats. You have a few choices, but the majority of this diet plan will require you to consume lean meats, eggs, and dairy products.

This diet will most likely differ from our usual eating habits. It may also contradict some of our health and fitness beliefs. It's extremely effective and has the potential to significantly improve our health. When you switch from an American diet to a carnivore diet, you'll notice a slew of health benefits:

Get in shape.

Carnivore diets are popular because they provide a sense of fulfillment.

I'm trying to slim down. One of your first thoughts when considering an all-meat diet is that it will cause you to gain weight. This has been demonstrated to be improbable. Cutting carbs out, similar to the ketogenic diet, will keep your blood sugar levels low. Insulin levels will not rise, and no calories will be stored as fat. Because of the restrictions on what you can eat, you may find it difficult to consume enough calories.

If you're someone who eats snacks like pretzels, nuts, and other snack foods out of control, the carnivore diet can help. You must prepare the food that you will eat because there isn't much room for snacks or even easy-to-prepare foods. When you consider how much effort it takes to prepare a meal, you'll learn to eat only when you're hungry.

Although it may appear to be simple to munch on the snacks without thinking, preparing a hamburger or steak is not an accident. To get the results you want, you'll have to put in some time and effort.

You'll discover how to eat only what you require and how to consume the necessary calories without feeling deprived. Above all, you'll learn to tell the difference between physiological hunger and mindless eating.

Many carnivores lose a lot of weight. They learn to eat only the foods that are good for them and avoid processed foods. All of these will help you lose weight by working together.

Boost the health of your heart

A carnivore diet can also benefit your heart. According to the Mayo Clinic, the cholesterol-to-total-cholesterol ratio is a better predictor of risk than LDL or total cholesterol. Take your total cholesterol and divide it by your HDL score to get this information. This will be determined by the results.

Your cholesterol should be taken into account as well. Doctors may consider higher LDL numbers to be dangerous, but knowing the type of LDL particles traveling through your veins is more important. Smaller, denser particles will be deemed more hazardous than larger, fluffier particles. Even if two people have the same LDL cholesterol level, their risks may differ.

According to the Cooper Institute, determining your HDL cholesterol to triglycerides ratio is the best way to figure out which type of LDL particles you have. Your risk will be reduced if this ratio is used.

For those who lived a carnivorous lifestyle, these ratios dropped. Despite the numerous debates and fears that this diet is unhealthy, the results have been incredible. Carnivore diets can both lower and raise cholesterol levels. You don't have to stop eating this way to reap the benefits.

This diet plan's advantages are also visible. It can help you keep your heart healthy by lowering your blood pressure and widening your arteries to allow more blood flow. These are just a few of the many advantages to your overall heart health that will help you live longer.

Can assist in the battle against diabetes

Many people are suffering from diabetes, which is rapidly becoming a major issue. This is a difficult condition to manage, and living a healthy lifestyle can be difficult. The good news is that by eating a carnivore diet, diabetes can be avoided or reduced.

When you eat too much sugar, you get diabetes. Diabetes is caused by eating too much sugar or carbs. The body will turn both of them into glucose. Despite the fact that glucose is the cells' preferred source of energy, too much of it can cause them to require less glucose.

Insulin is produced by the liver to tell the cells when it's time to take in glucose. If you eat healthily, this process will be successful. Your cells may become insulin resistant if you consume too much glucose. To recognize that it exists, the cells will require more insulin. The liver will continue to produce insulin, and the cells' sensitivity will improve.

Insulin won't be recognized as a substance by the cells for a long time. Despite the fact that there will be plenty of glucose available and the cells will still require it, the insulin-sensitive cells will refuse to absorb it. Blood sugar levels that are too high can cause serious health complications. People will feel exhausted and worn down if they do not get the nutrients they require.

Following a carnivore lifestyle can help to solve this problem. You will no longer need to consume as many insulins as you once did. You will only consume animal products instead of carbohydrates. This increases the sensitivity of the cells to insulin, allowing them to absorb more glucose that had previously been unused.

This diet plan can help your cells regain insulin sensitivity if followed correctly. It can also aid in the reduction or elimination of diabetes symptoms. This diet plan may be more effective than taking numerous harmful medications or worrying about high blood sugar levels in dealing with diabetes and other issues.Inflammation issues are reduced.

Inflammation will impact a large number of people. It is one of the primary causes of many of today's health issues. Finding ways to reduce inflammation can make a significant difference in our overall health.

Some vegans believe that consuming too many animal-based foods that are high in fat causes inflammation. Many argue that eating animal products can cause just as much inflammation as smoking cigarettes.

Inflammation can be reduced by eating these foods. Subjects were compared, according to a 2013 study published in the journal Metabolism. Participants were split into two groups: high-fat, low-carb eaters and high-carb, low-fat eaters. Both groups' calories were reduced after 12 weeks, and high-fat eaters' inflammation markers were reduced.

According to the findings of this study, eating more fats and less carbohydrates may have a greater impact on heart health and inflammation reduction.

It occurs for this reason. CRP is produced by the liver in response to inflammation. CRP levels in the blood can be used to determine the severity of your inflammation. It is considered normal to have a CRP level of 10 mg/L. A CRP level of less than 1 mg/L, on the other hand, is regarded as excellent.

High-fat participants' blood levels were checked, and their CRP levels were found to be extremely low. 0.34 was the average. This is a significant figure, indicating that a low-carb diet combined with a high-fat diet may be the key to reducing inflammation. It may also assist us in achieving our desired health outcomes, such as lower blood pressure, diabetes, and cholesterol levels.

testosterone levels higher

Some people who have tried the carnivore diet claim that their testosterone levels have increased. Healthy fats have been shown to increase testosterone levels in people of all ages in studies. Men who ate low-fiber, high-fat diets for at least ten weeks had a 13 percent increase in testosterone levels compared to those who ate low-fat, low-fiber diets, according to a study published in the American Journal of Clinical Nutrition.

Reading up on the diet and how it can help you improve your fertility might be worthwhile. There are numerous benefits to this diet plan. It can even help men who have been struggling with low testosterone levels.

If you have low testosterone levels and are having difficulty getting results at the gym, or if your sex life is suffering, a testosterone boost may be beneficial. To increase your testosterone, you don't need to spend a lot of money on drugs. If you want to achieve the results you want, you don't have to stop eating meat and switch to a carnivore diet.

HDL cholesterol levels are increased.

Cholesterol is divided into two groups. LDL cholesterol is the carrier of cholesterol from the liver to the rest of the body. This is the most dangerous type of cholesterol, which is why most people try to avoid it. To maintain your health, you should keep this number as low as possible.

HDL cholesterol, on the other hand, is a good type of cholesterol. The cholesterol will be removed from the body and stored in the liver. So that cholesterol does not harm the body, the liver can reuse or eliminate it.

If you follow a carnivore diet, your triglyceride levels will fall. Your HDL levels, on the other hand, will go up. The triglyceride HDL/triglyceride ratio is a strong indication of heart disease.

This ratio indicates a higher risk of heart disease. The carnivore diet can help to reduce this ratio, and it can be beneficial to your body in a variety of ways.

control of hunger

When you switch to a carnivore lifestyle, you'll be surprised at how much you feel less hungry. If you stick to this diet, you won't feel deprived or have a lot of unhealthy food cravings. For the first week, as your body adjusts to not eating as much, it will be challenging. You'll be able to control your appetite and stop eating junk food as frequently after that.

Intermittent fasting is a popular option for carnivores. This satisfies their hunger and allows them to go longer between meals. This is much easier than other diets because your stomach won't rumble and you won't have to try to persuade it to eat all the delicious but unhealthy foods you love.

For those who are concerned about hunger or dislike the idea of following a diet, the carnivore diet is a viable option. You'll be able to eat more and feel fuller faster with this diet plan. This will make you feel more fulfilled while also assisting you in losing weight more quickly.

Digestion issues are less common.

When people begin the carnivore diet, they are concerned about their bodies' ability to provide the required amount of fiber. Fiber is said to be important for our overall health. Fiber is important to our digestive system, according to advertisements for Metamucil or bran muffins. When you're a carnivore, fiber might be more trouble than it's worth. This could be true, even if science proves otherwise.

Researchers looked into the effects of reducing fiber intake on chronic constipation in a study published in the World Journal of Gastroenterology in 2012. This goes against everything we've learned about constipation in the past, as well as what many doctors advise.

During the study, the participants were told to consume little fiber. They were able to gradually increase their fiber intake after the two-week period until they reached their desired level of comfort. If they wanted to, they could even eat a high-fiber diet.

Surprisingly, many participants reported feeling better after following the zero-fiber plan. All of this occurred over a six-month period. Their health did not significantly improve as a result of the high-fiber diet. Those who ate no fiber or a low amount of fiber, on the other hand, experienced a slight improvement in symptoms like bloating, gas, and straining. People who were deficient in fiber had more bowel movements per day.

What makes you think that? In order to improve digestion, you can eat less fiber or even none at all. Fiber is said to improve the efficiency of your digestive system.

Many people's stomachs and why fiber-rich foods can cause problems are still unknown. Many carnivores will blame plant-based compounds for their digestive issues. The Plant Paradox, by Steven R. Gundry, M.D., claims that plants' natural defense mechanisms can cause gas, bloating, and other digestive issues, making them unfit for human consumption.

It's critical to avoid certain plants to ensure that fiber and other nutrients don't cause your body to react negatively. Seeds, nuts, and beans should be avoided if at all possible. They have the potential to cause inflammation and auto-immune diseases in the body.

This is a controversial viewpoint, but it may explain why many carnivores claim they feel better when they eat meat rather than plants. For a long time, we've all been told that fiber is necessary for good health and that we should consume it. This may not be the case. The carnivore diet has been discussed, and it will test a lot of our assumptions.

Blood pressure is reduced.

If you've ever had to deal with high blood pressure, you understand the importance of lowering it and keeping yourself healthy. If your blood pressure continues to rise, your heart health and overall health may suffer.

High blood pressure can indicate the onset of heart disease in the future. Following a carnivore diet can help you lower your blood pressure. Following the ketogenic diet can help you lower your blood pressure. You may even be able to get off your blood pressure medication.

To lower blood pressure, a variety of medications are available. While some of these medications may be effective, the majority of them will not provide you with the desired results. Even those who work can have side effects that are worse than hypertension. They have the potential to make a lot of people sicker.

To lower your high blood pressure, you can make dietary changes. The carnivore diet is the most successful at lowering these figures. This diet plan will assist you in lowering your salt intake, reducing your consumption of processed and fast foods, and encouraging you to eat more healthily. When all of these factors are combined, you'll notice dramatic improvements in your health and blood pressure.

Extra vigor

Glycogen is a limited resource in the human body. You'll need to replenish your glycogen stores from time to time to maintain your energy levels. The vast majority of people have enough fat in their bodies to keep them going. The body will never run out of fat because it has more storage capacity than glycogen.

Consider how much more energy you'd have if you ate well. Many people believe that fat is bad for you and that you should avoid it at all costs. Healthy fats, on the other hand, will provide you with more energy over time.

We all want to be able to do more things with our time. We seem to be trying to do too much all of the time. It's easy to run out of energy and feel as if you can't keep up with the daily grind of work, housecleaning, kids getting home from school, appointments, visiting friends, and everything else.

To get through the day, people will drink a lot of coffee and energy drinks. These can be effective for a short period of time, but they frequently go bad much faster than we would like. This can result in a significant drop in our mood and make us feel even worse. These aren't the most effective methods for gaining or maintaining energy.

The carnivore diet is an excellent way to get the right amount of energy at the right time without experiencing any abrupt energy drops. As your body adjusts to the new diet, the first week may be a little rough. Once you make the necessary changes, you will be surprised at how much natural energy you have.

Mental clarity is improved

As you can see, people who live a carnivore lifestyle have more mental clarity and focus. When you first start this diet, you may notice that your body needs to adjust. If you were a high-carb eater before starting the diet plan, this period of adjustment will be more difficult. During this time, you may experience symptoms such as brain fog, moodiness, and fatigue.

While adjusting to the ketogenic diet, some people experience other side effects. It's possible that you'll have difficulty sleeping or that your breath will smell bad. This means your body is making ketones and you're in ketosis. This will cause your energy levels to rise.

If you can keep it up for at least a week, the side effects will fade. You will notice that your mind is clearer and that you have more energy after this period.

It's a more straightforward method of weight loss.

The carnivore lifestyle is simple, which is something everyone can agree on. When you're hungry, you eat animal food. This diet plan is for you if you dislike the idea of a diet or its complexity, if you're confused about calories and macros, and if you don't want to spend your life weighing food portions on a scale. Dieting is made simple by the fact that there are so few things to remember.

You don't have to measure anything with this diet plan. It's simple to eat only when you're hungry and stop when your stomach hurts. You can look over the food and measure the portions if you're curious. It will be much easier to stick to the diet plan if your body can communicate with you.

This diet plan will not limit your eating habits. This diet allows you to consume a low-carbohydrate, high-fat diet. These fats help you eat fewer calories by filling you up. When you stick to this diet plan, you'll feel full and satisfied. This is how you will be able to shed pounds.

Eating a carnivore diet has a number of health benefits. It won't be like anything you've ever experienced before. Once you've become familiar with the carnivore diet and the rules for what you can and cannot eat, it'll be easy to stick to it. Learning the rules is simple, and your health will improve as a result.

Is the Diet Plan in any way problematic?

The carnivore diet appears to be similar to the ketogenic diet, and we've already established that meat isn't the only cause of heart disease. Most people, at least in the short term, should be able to benefit from this type of diet.

There are a lot of misconceptions about all-meat diets and how they affect your health. The good news is that many of these urban legends are false and unsupported by science. Consider the idea that meat can go undigested in the intestines or other parts of the stomach.

This myth has been around for a long time and may be something that vegans and vegetarians should think about. It's ridiculous to believe that red meat will sit in your stomach undigested. Meat, like all other foods, is absorbed first in the small intestine before moving on to the colon. Meat can't stay unabsorbed in the GI tract, which is a myth.

Certain circumstances in our lives can cause bowel obstruction. A disease or a physical injury are examples of this. The gastrointestinal tract is not obstructed by red meat. Smaller bowel movements may lead people to believe that there isn't a lot of waste coming out at once.

Smaller movements, including those seen in carnivores, are caused by consuming low levels of fiber. Fiber will help to bulk things up a bit. Because you're not eating as many fruits and vegetables, your bowel movements are smaller.

This isn't always a negative aspect. When you stick to a carnivore diet, you won't get constipated or have any other problems. You'll have regular bowel movements. It doesn't matter if you have a lot of bowel movements or if you eat red meat.

Many people who tried the carnivore diet found that they didn't experience any water retention, bloating, or distension. They felt lighter and more energized after starting the diet than they had before.

A carnivore diet can increase your chances of getting cancer. Phytonutrients found in plant foods have been shown in numerous studies to protect DNA and help prevent diseases like cancer. These foods can harm your health in the long run, and if you don't eat them, you may be more likely to develop cancer.

Bacteria in our stomachs, GI tracts, and colons ferment fiber into butyrate. This fatty acid can help to lower our risk of colon cancer by reducing inflammation in the gastrointestinal tract. Patients who eat a carnivore diet are discouraged by experts.

Research also backs up the opposing viewpoint. Many people have found that following a ketogenic diet similar to the one shown here is an effective way to manage their cancer. It could even be used to treat chemotherapy patients, making them feel more at ease during their treatment. However, it appears that more research is required to determine how effective this diet plan will be over time.

It's worth noting that while some doctors believe an all-animal diet like this increases your risk of colon cancer, this isn't because they believe animal foods are carcinogenic. The problem isn't with the foods you eat, but with the foods you choose to avoid. It will be impossible to consume foods that aid in the prevention of colon cancer. When you cut out so many fruits and vegetables, fighting cancer becomes very difficult. It's not all bad when it comes to red meat. It simply means that your body isn't getting enough of the nutrients it requires to stay healthy.

People are concerned about the effects of this diet plan on their gut biome, or the bacteria that aid in digestion and disease prevention. The flora (bad bacteria) that was being followed was unaffected by the diet plan. Beneficial flora was also in greater abundance.

This is because the carnivore diet is a good way to get rid of toxins. It will starve all sugar-hungry bacteria because you don't eat carbs or sugars. Some beneficial bacteria may also perish as a result. Perhaps we don't require as many as we believe. If we eat a diet rich in plant foods, we might not require as many.

More people will be interested in learning more about the carnivore diet, despite the fact that this is a topic that has not been thoroughly explored.

The carnivore diet is generally considered to be healthy, and it is unlikely to result in serious vitamin or mineral deficiencies. If someone follows the diet correctly and consumes enough healthy nutrients, it is not difficult to maintain.

Iron and zinc are plentiful in red meat. Seafood and dairy, which are commonly added to plant foods, contain the vitamin D your body requires. If you don't eat plants, you'll have the most trouble getting vitamin C. There are, however, a variety of other ways to consume this nutrient.

Some carnivore advocates will argue that if you don't eat carbs, you don't need as much vitamin A as if you eat the fruits and vegetables. Even small amounts of vitamin A can be used well. In fact, there is some speculation that the ketone known as beta-hydroxybutyrate, which your body is going to start producing naturally when you take the carbs out of the diet, can help to replace the need for vitamin C, at least in part.

A balanced diet will have vitamin C play a role in the formation of collagen. However, it is possible to get the same effect from the amino acids found in meat, so you don't need to consume the produce. No one has ever reported that they got scurvy from this diet.

You must ensure that you include a variety of animal foods in your diet. Do not limit yourself to eating one type or food every day. As with any diet, if you eat only hamburgers every night, your body will not get enough nutrients. You can ensure your body receives the nutrients it needs by eating a variety of foods, even if you are following a carnivore diet.

Missing out on the nutrients

Most people who opt to eat a carnivore diet will still be able get the nutrients and vitamins they need. It will surprise you at the number of vitamins and minerals that can be found in different meat sources. Although we've been told for many years that eating fruits and vegetables is the best way to get minerals, most of them can be found in animal products and protein.

It is important to eat lots of different foods. You won't be able to enjoy as many different foods as you want if you only eat steak every night. To ensure you get all the nutrients, you need to explore all the options for animal products. You can get all the nutrients you need from meat, poultry, bacon, turkey, fish, and other animal products.

Despite this, some people have difficulty getting the nutrients they need from this diet plan. It's often because they don't follow the diet plan correctly and stick to one type of meat. They don't include variety in their meals, and end up eating the same two to three recipes every day. It is difficult to give the body the nutrients it needs. This can lead to some problems, which could prove very costly.

You may have nutrient deficiencies if you don't want to spend the time to search for many recipes that use different animal products. This is true for any diet plan. Traditional American diets are often full of unhealthy foods. Participants can also suffer from nutrient deficiencies and a lack of variety. To keep your body healthy, follow the rules of the carnivore lifestyle and include as many animal products as you can.Is there anyone who shouldn't follow a carnivore's diet?

A carnivore meal is possible for the average person. If you take the proper steps and get all of the nutrients you require, you can live a healthy lifestyle. If you add variety to your diet, you will lose weight and gain better health.

These dangers should be understood by those who are not suitable for a carnivore diet. For children under the age of twelve, this diet is not recommended. This type of diet should be used with caution by teenagers. For children under the age of 13, this diet plan is not recommended by a doctor. These older people need a wide variety of nutrients. Animal products provide them with only a fraction of the nutrition they require.

Women who are pregnant or nursing should exercise caution when following a carnivore diet. Pregnant and nursing women, like teenagers and children, will need more nutrition than animal products can provide. If you think the carnivore lifestyle is right for you, consult your physician first. This will enable you to determine whether or not you have any health problems.

If you have any health concerns, you should speak with your physician. If you choose to follow this diet, some health conditions may become too difficult to manage. If you have any medical conditions, you should always seek medical advice to ensure your safety and health.

Is a carnivore diet suitable for athletes?

Those who believe that carbs are necessary for a healthy body if you exercise regularly have already criticized the ketogenic diet. Science has repeatedly demonstrated that you can exercise and perform at an elite level while following a low-carb diet.

All plant foods and carbs are avoided on the carnivore diet. The ketogenic or other low-carb diets do not require you to completely eliminate carbs. You can, however, eat some of them. Carnivores will consume very few carbohydrates. When it comes to doing intense workouts, this can be problematic. When following this type of diet, there are a few other considerations to keep in mind.

The short answer to the question is as follows: We don't know how the carnivore diet will affect people in the long run. We also can't say how it'll affect endurance, performance, or muscle mass. Despite having to cut back on their carb intake, many dieters who have tried the carnivore diet report seeing significant gains in endurance and muscle mass. Some people said they gained more weight on this diet than on any other.

It's important to remember that transitioning from a traditional American diet to a carnivore diet will leave you exhausted.

It's possible that your body won't be able to get the steady supply of carbs and glucose it requires. It may take some time to adjust to fats as a source of energy. For the first few weeks, you might find it beneficial to cut back on your workouts. Allowing your body to adjust and rest before attempting to increase your gains is a good idea.

Furthermore, weightlifting accounted for the majority of the gains. There hasn't been a lot of research done to see how cardio will fare. Carnivore diet may be difficult for people who do a lot of exercise. This is due to the fact that fat does not convert to fuel quickly enough to handle the intense cardio and movements required. It may be necessary to cut back on your cardio or find another form of exercise that will help you gain strength without burning too much fuel.

If you're a serious athlete who is dedicated to his or her training, you may want to make some changes to your carnivore diet to ensure you get the nutrition you need to fuel your body and achieve your objectives. The traditional carnivore lifestyle is best for those who only exercise once in a while or are content with shorter workouts.

What part of the Carnivore Diet does exercise play?

Let's see if the carnivore diet is suitable and acceptable for people who like to exercise. It's natural to wonder whether this diet will require you to exercise or if you'll be able to stick to your current exercise routine. This chapter will go over how exercise fits into the carnivore lifestyle and provide additional information on this amazing diet.

Helping Athletes with a Carnivorous Diet

When following the ketogenic diet, many bodybuilders have noticed that their athletic performance suffers. Although you can follow a targeted ketogenic or cyclical diet to achieve your goals, many athletes prefer to eat a carnivore diet.

Many athletes are succeeding in their attempts to eat only meat. These people are experiencing positive results, and it's possible that this way of eating will become the norm in the future.

Despite the fact that the carnivore lifestyle has been around for centuries, few studies have been conducted to prove that it is the best diet for athletes to improve their performance. Many people may benefit from this type of diet, according to evidence.

This is the idea that increasing your daily protein intake (which is what happens when athletes adopt a carnivore lifestyle) will provide enough sugar (which can happen to protein through the process of glucoseogenesis) to improve your performance.

For many bodybuilders, this is great news. To finish intense workouts and build muscle and strength, these bodybuilders often require some glucose and sugars. The ketogenic diet was created with a targeted and cyclical approach in mind.

It is preferable to ensure that you are getting enough protein rather than cheating on the carnivore diet by adding extra sugars or carbs at certain times. The gluconeogenesis process can then convert this to sugar.

The carnivore diet will provide small amounts of glucose rather than relying solely on ketones as a source of energy, as low-carb diets do. You'll have enough glucose to fuel your body for anaerobic exercises like weightlifting or bodybuilding.

One thing to keep in mind about the carnivore diet is that if you follow the rules, your body will produce more collagen. Collagen is essential for joint and muscle recovery after strenuous exercise. Collagen is a protein that binds everything in your body, including your skin and joints. To ensure that everything works properly, it must be plentiful.

Many people doubt the health benefits of a carnivore diet. They believe it is also harmful to their health. We've been told for years that whole grains and fruits and vegetables are necessary components of a healthy diet. We will be hungry and tired if we do not consume them, and our athletic performance will suffer as a result.

This may be the primary reason why people are hesitant to adopt a carnivore lifestyle. They are afraid of losing any of their gains, and they do not want this to occur. These claims, however, appear to be supported by evidence and research. If you live a carnivore lifestyle, your gains will skyrocket.

Many people have had great success by adopting a carnivore diet. It's simple to become accustomed to the food you must consume in order to avoid cheating.

What about cardiovascular exercises?

If you enjoy doing intense cardio, you may need to reduce your workouts. Most people are unaffected by this. You can easily incorporate some cardio into your workouts. If you enjoy running for an hour every day and aren't willing to take it slowly, the carnivore diet might not be for you.

Cardio is a time-consuming and energy-intensive activity. Carbohydrates are required for the proper functioning of your body. Glucose is a simple sugar that can be quickly broken down and used. This enables us to continue working out longer and harder. Although fat is beneficial for strength training, it cannot provide the energy needed for cardio quickly enough.

If you enjoy doing intense workouts, you may need to modify your diet. It's possible that you'll need to switch up your diet plan.

The good news is that not everyone will have to exert as much effort to complete their tasks. They'll still be able to eat meat, but they'll be able to do some cardio as well. If you keep a healthy cardio level and don't push yourself too hard, this plan will work for you.

HIIT training is another option if you want to get a good workout while on a carnivore diet. High-intensity interval training is also known as HIIT. It allows you to work hard for a minute and then take a five-minute break. A few rounds will provide you with a good workout.

Up-and-down cycles are more effective than a long, intense workout, according to research. Even if you follow a carnivore diet, it will still work.

Is it possible to achieve results without working out?

The best part about the carnivore lifestyle is that you can see results even if you don't spend a lot of time in the gym or at home. The carnivore lifestyle is extremely efficient, despite its appearance being far more impressive than other diets.

On its own, the carnivore diet is very effective. You'll get a lot more good nutrients and eat a lot less bad. You can cut back on processed foods and baked goods while also reducing your intake of animal products. Because these foods are high in calories, cutting them out will significantly reduce the number of calories you consume.

If you stick to the diet plan and eat only when you're hungry, you'll be able to cut down on the amount of food you consume. The majority of the animal products you'll need to consume on this diet are filling. You can eat fewer or smaller meals as a result of this. This will aid in your health improvement.

You will benefit from the fact that a carnivore diet allows you to lose weight. In order to achieve ketosis, your body now relies on the fats you eat. If you stick to this kind of diet, this is the only way your body will get energy. Both the fats you eat and the fats stored in your body can be burned very effectively by your body.

You'll lose weight while remaining energetic and satisfied. The carnivore lifestyle can aid weight loss even if you don't exercise every day.

Regardless of how effective a carnivore's diet is, getting some exercise at least a few times per week is always a good idea. Rather than sitting on the couch, you should exercise your heart and muscles. This diet plan may also aid in the improvement of your health and the attainment of better results. Regardless of whether you do cardio, strength training, or a combination of both, you should work out at least three to four days per week. This diet plan will assist you in achieving your desired results without having to visit the gym.

Is it necessary for me to slow down now and then?

You might need to take it easy at times. Your body may not be ready for the changes you'll be making once you start eating carnivores. You may feel exhausted and worn down as a result of this. It is preferable not to overwork yourself and attempt to accomplish too much.

When you're first starting out on a carnivore diet, it's best to relax and take a deep breath. During this time, you don't want to overwork yourself. Your body has spent so much time adjusting to the diet that it is unsure what to do when the glucose is taken away. Withdrawal symptoms and irritability are possible side effects.

This diet plan may not be right for you if you've ever struggled with sugar addiction. Not only will you have to deal with glucose withdrawal symptoms and the other issues that can arise from your body not receiving a consistent supply of energy, but you will also have to deal with withdrawal symptoms.

For the first few weeks of this diet, you should take it slowly. You can work around your hectic schedule or take a week off. You can take a break from your workout routine or schedule it for a less busy time.

After a few weeks, you should notice an increase in energy levels. When compared to traditional diets, healthy fats will provide you with significantly more energy. The body's fat source takes a long time to convert to fuel. Set aside some time for yourself.

Suggestions for a More Successful Carnivore Diet

There are many aspects of a carnivore lifestyle that you will enjoy. It's simple to follow because you only need to be familiar with a few foods and a few food groups. You don't have to consume a lot of food to get all of the vitamins and minerals your body requires. It'll be delectable. For meat lovers, this is the ideal diet plan.

The carnivore diet will be unlike anything you've ever had before. The carnivore diet is more restrictive than other diets, regardless of whether you've tried them before. To get the best results, there are a number of tips and tricks you can use:

Join a friend on the diet plan.

Any type of diet plan can be difficult to stick to. When it comes to living a carnivore lifestyle, you'll be asked to stick to a few foods. Any type of meat, including fatty meats and eggs, is permitted. All other food groups must be eliminated. This can be difficult for people who have poor eating habits, especially those who eat a lot of bread and pasta.

Having a friend join you on this diet can make a significant difference. While adhering to this diet plan, you will both have similar experiences. This means that you can support each other. You can encourage each other to work towards your goal, call each others for support, share recipes, etc.

Do not attempt to go on a carnivore diet on your own. Consider finding a\sA friend, or even an online support group, can help you to get your diet plan in order.

Slowly start to eliminate the foods

Some people find that the carnivore diet works best when they go cold turkey. They pick a day to start the diet and then go crazy. They eliminate all dairy, grains, and produce on that day. They also eliminate all processed and baked goods they can enjoy.

They find that cheating even a little is enough to cause them problems. These people may struggle to control themselves and will not be able stop once they start. These people may find it difficult to jump in and not look back. Otherwise, they will fail.

Others find it too difficult to jump all the way from the beginning. They might be concerned about their health if they eliminate all food groups at once. They may want to ease into the process so that they don't cause too much shock. It doesn't matter what reason they have, it is okay to slowly eliminate foods.

You don't have to give up all your favorite foods at once. Start by eliminating one food group each week until you reach the carnivore diet. Others have also found that the ketogenic diet can be helpful, starting with it and gradually moving on to something else when they feel ready.

Relax during the adjustment time

You should take a break during the first week of your carnivore diet. You don't have to be excited about losing weight or seeing results. It will be difficult to start the carnivore lifestyle. You may feel exhausted and tired. You should not rush into the diet and get too excited about it. This can cause you to feel more tired and make it difficult to stick with it.

When you are starting this type of diet, the best thing you can do is to relax. You shouldn't jump into this type of diet plan if you are having a hectic week or are dealing with a lot of stress. It is important to be able to relax while on the diet, especially at the beginning.

This could work best if you can take a week off. You can rest and take naps and not feel stressed about the work or activities you have to do during this time. You may be able limit the work you do during this time, but you might not be able. You can wait until the end of a major project to work remotely, but you should not do so.

While there are many benefits to this diet plan, and it will make you feel great, the first week can be difficult. Your body will adjust to the new fuel source. Your favorite foods may have to be cut out, even if they were healthy. You will also experience a lot more cravings for carbs and sugars. All of this will make you feel grumpy and moody.

It is best not to add too much work to these changes in your emotions or how you feel. It is easy to see why you might be better off completing a major project at work first, waiting until things slow down, taking a break and working from home so you can recuperate and adjust to the new diet plan.Is there anybody who should avoid following a carnivorous diet?

A carnivorous supper is within reach of the typical individual. If you take the proper measures and receive all of the nutrients you need, you can be healthy. If you add diversity to your diet, you will lose weight and enhance your health.

These dangers should be understood by those who are not suited to a carnivorous diet. This diet is not suitable for children under the age of 12. This sort of diet should be avoided by teenagers. A doctor does not suggest this eating plan for children under the age of 13. These people in their latter years need a broad variety of nutrients. Animal products are tough for them to get the nourishment they need.

Women who are pregnant or breastfeeding should be careful while eating a carnivorous diet. Pregnant and breastfeeding women, like teens and toddlers, will need more nourishment than animal products can provide. If you think the carnivorous lifestyle is suited for you, consult with your doctor first. This can help you figure out whether you have any health problems.

If you have any health concerns, you should speak with your doctor. If you choose to follow this diet, you may find it challenging to manage certain health concerns. If you have any medical issues, you should always visit your doctor to guarantee your safety and health.

Is it possible for athletes to consume a carnivorous diet?

The ketogenic diet has previously been slammed by critics, as have others who feel that carbohydrates are important for a healthy body if you exercise frequently. Science has consistently shown that you can exercise while following a low-carb diet and still perform at an exceptional level.

All plant items and carbohydrates are eliminated from the carnivorous diet. The ketogenic or other low-carb diets do not need you to remove all carbohydrates. You may, however, consume some of it. Carnivores consume practically no carbohydrates. When it comes to doing intensive exercises, this might cause some problems. When following this sort of diet plan, there are a few more things to keep in mind.

This is a quick response to the question. We don't know what the carnivorous diet's long-term consequences will be. We also don't know how it will influence endurance, performance, or muscle mass. Despite needing to reduce their carb consumption, many dieters who have tried the carnivore diet report seeing significant increases in endurance and muscle growth. Some participants said that they gained more weight on this diet than on any other.

One thing to keep in mind is that transitioning from a regular American diet to a carnivorous diet can leave you exhausted.

It's possible that your body won't be able to get the continuous quantity of carbs and glucose it requires. It might take some time to become used to consuming fats as a source of energy. For the first few weeks, you may find it advantageous to minimize the number of exercises you complete. Before you attempt to enhance your gains, give your body time to acclimate and recover.

Weightlifting was also responsible for the bulk of the improvements. There hasn't been a lot of study done on how cardio will perform. People who engage in a lot of physical activity may struggle with the carnivorous diet. This is due to the fact that fat does not convert to fuel rapidly enough to manage the intensity of cardio and the requisite motions. It may be important to lessen your cardio or find another kind of training that allows you to increase strength without burning too much fuel.

If you're a serious athlete who is dedicated to his or her training, you may want to make some modifications to your carnivorous diet to ensure you obtain the nutrients you need to power your body and reach your objectives. The conventional carnivorous lifestyle is excellent for folks who just exercise once in a while or prefer shorter exercises.

What role does exercise play in the Carnivore Diet?

Next, consider if a carnivorous diet is appropriate and acceptable for folks who like working out. It's natural to ask if this diet will demand you to exercise or whether you'll be able to stick to your current fitness program. This chapter will go over how exercise fits into the carnivorous lifestyle and provide you more details on this amazing diet.

The Carnivore Diet and Athletes

Many bodybuilders have discovered that when they adopt a ketogenic diet, their physical performance suffers. Although a tailored ketogenic or cyclical diet is an option, many athletes choose to consume a carnivorous diet to reach their objectives.

Many athletes are attempting to consume only meat and reporting positive outcomes. These people are having a lot of success, and it's feasible that this way of eating may become the standard in the future.

Despite the fact that the carnivorous lifestyle has been around for hundreds of years, few research have been conducted to establish that it is the greatest diet for athletes to increase their performance. Many individuals may benefit from this sort of diet, according to research.

This is the belief that increasing your daily protein consumption (which is what occurs when athletes adopt a carnivorous diet) would offer enough sugar (which can happen to protein via the process of glucoseogenesis) to boost your performance.

For many bodybuilders, this is fantastic news. To complete tough exercises and grow muscle and strength, these bodybuilders often need glucose and carbohydrates. The ketogenic diet was created with both targeted and cyclical goals in mind.

It is preferable to ensure that you are receiving adequate protein rather than straying on the carnivorous diet by adding additional sweets or carbohydrates at certain times. Gluconeogenesis may then be used to turn this into sugar.

Rather of depending only on ketones for energy, as low-carb diets do, the carnivore diet will give tiny quantities of glucose. You'll have enough glucose to power your body for anaerobic activity like weightlifting or bodybuilding.

One thing to keep in mind about the carnivorous lifestyle is that if you follow the rules, your body will produce more collagen. Collagen aids in the rehabilitation of joints and muscles after strenuous exercise. Collagen is a protein that holds everything in your body together, from your skin to your joints. It must be plenty to guarantee that everything runs well.

Many individuals are suspicious about the health advantages of a carnivorous diet. They also feel it is harmful to their health. We've been told for years that whole grains and fruits and vegetables are vital components of a healthy diet. We will feel hungry and exhausted without them, and our athletic performance will decrease.

This might be the primary reason why individuals are hesitant to adopt a carnivorous diet. They are afraid of losing any of their gains, and they do not want this to happen. The data and study, on the other hand, seem to back up these statements. If you live a carnivorous lifestyle, your gains will rise.

Many individuals have reaped incredible benefits from adopting a carnivorous diet. It's simple to get used to the meals you must consume and prevent cheating.

What about the cardiovascular system?

If you prefer intensive cardio, you may need to cut down on your exercises. For the most part, this isn't an issue. You can still include some cardio into your training without difficulty. If you like jogging for an hour every day and aren't willing to take it gradually, the carnivore diet may not be for you.

Cardio is a time-consuming exercise that takes a great deal of work and energy. Carbohydrates are required to power your body. Glucose is readily digestible and may be utilized right away. This permits us to continue working out for longer periods of time and at a higher intensity. Although fat is beneficial for strength training, it cannot deliver the energy required for cardio rapidly enough.

If you like doing rigorous exercises, you may need to change your diet. It's possible that you'll need to switch to a new eating plan.

The good news is that not everyone will have to work as hard to complete their tasks. They'll still be allowed to eat meat, but they'll also be able to perform some exercise. If you keep a decent cardio level and don't push yourself too hard, this approach will work.

HIIT exercise is another option if you want to work out hard while on a carnivorous diet. High-intensity interval training (HIIT) is another name for HIIT. It enables you to work hard for roughly a minute before taking a five-minute break. A couple rounds will give you a tremendous workout.

Up-and-down cycles have been shown in studies to be more beneficial than a protracted, hard exercise. If you're on a carnivorous diet, it'll still function.

Are there any outcomes if you don't do the workouts?

The greatest part of living a carnivorous diet is that you can notice results even if you don't spend a lot of time at the gym or at home. The carnivorous lifestyle is incredibly efficient, despite the fact that it seems to be significantly more impressive than certain other diets.

On its own, the carnivorous diet is quite effective. You'll receive a lot more beneficial nutrients, and you'll consume a lot less bad things. You can cut down on processed meals and baked items while reducing your intake of animal products. Because these items are heavy in calories, cutting them out will substantially lower the number of calories you consume.

If you stick to the diet plan and eat just when you're hungry, you'll be able to cut down on your food intake. The bulk of the animal items you'll need to consume on this diet plan will be satisfying. This implies you may eat fewer or smaller meals as a result. This will assist you in improving your health.

You will benefit from the fact that you may lose weight by following a carnivorous diet. To achieve ketosis, your body now relies on the fats you consume. If you follow this food plan, this is the only way your body will acquire energy. Both the fats you consume and the fats stored in your body may be burned extremely effectively by your body.

You will reduce weight while remaining energetic and satisfied. The carnivorous lifestyle may help you lose weight even if you don't exercise every day.

Regardless matter how effective a carnivore's diet is, it is always advisable to obtain some activity at least a few times each week. You should not just sit on the sofa but also move your heart and muscles. This diet plan may also aid in the improvement of your health and the attainment of better outcomes. Whether you do cardio, strength training, or a mix of the two, you should work out at least three to four days a week. This eating plan will allow you to achieve your goals without having to go to the gym.

Is it necessary for me to take it easy on occasion?

You may need to take it easy at times. Your body may not be ready for the adjustments you'll be making once you start eating carnivores. This might make you feel exhausted and worn out. It is preferable not to overwork oneself and strive to do too much.

When you're starting the carnivore diet, it's advisable to relax and take a big breath. During this moment, you don't want to push yourself too hard. Your body has spent so much time adapting to the diet that it doesn't know what to do when the glucose is removed. Withdrawal symptoms and moodiness are possible.

You should also be aware that if you've ever struggled with sugar addiction, this diet plan may not be right for you. You'll have to cope with not just glucose withdrawal symptoms and the other issues that might arise when your body isn't getting enough energy, but also withdrawal symptoms.

For the first several weeks of this diet, you should take it easy. Work may be scheduled around your hectic schedule, or you can take a week off. You may take a vacation from your training program or plan it for a more convenient time.

After the first few weeks, you will feel an increase in energy levels. Healthy fats will provide you with far more energy than typical diets. It takes a long time for the body's fat stores to turn into fuel. Allow yourself some time.

Tips for a More Successful Carnivore Diet

There are many aspects of the carnivorous lifestyle that you will like. It's simple to follow since you only need to know a few foods and a few food types. You don't have to consume a lot to receive all the vitamins and minerals your body requires. It'll be delicious. For meat eaters, this is the ideal diet plan.

The carnivore diet will be unlike anything you've ever eaten before. Regardless of whether you've tried other diets, the carnivore diet is more restrictive than others. To get the greatest results, you may apply the following tips and tricks:

Participate in the diet plan with a pal.

It might be challenging to stick to any diet regimen. When it comes to the carnivorous lifestyle, you'll be urged to stick to a small number of meals. You are free to consume whatever kind of meat you choose, including fatty meats and eggs. All other food categories will have to be avoided. For people who have unhealthy eating habits, especially those who enjoy bread and spaghetti, this might be challenging.

Having a buddy accompany you on this diet may make a huge impact. While following this eating plan, you will have the same sensations. This means you'll be able to help each other. You can motivate each other to achieve your goal by calling each other for support, sharing recipes, and so on.

You should not attempt a carnivore diet on your own. Consider enlisting the help of a friend or an online support group to help you get your diet in order.

Begin removing the foods one by one.

Some people find that going cold turkey on the carnivore diet works best for them. They choose a day to begin the diet and then go berserk. On that day, they don't eat any dairy, grains, or produce. They also cut out all processed and baked goods from their diet.

They've discovered that even a small amount of cheating is enough to cause them problems. These individuals may struggle to maintain self-control and will be unable to stop once they begin. It may be difficult for these individuals to jump in and not look back. They will fail if they do not do so.

Others find starting from the beginning to be too difficult. If they eliminate all food groups at once, they may be concerned about their health. They may want to take it slowly at first to avoid causing too much shock. It's fine to gradually eliminate foods for whatever reason they have.

You are not obligated to give up all of your favorite foods all at once. Begin by removing one food group per week until you've reached the carnivore diet. Others have found that starting with the ketogenic diet and gradually moving on to something else when they are ready has been beneficial.

During the adjustment period, take it easy.

During the first week of your carnivore diet, you should take a break. You don't have to be overjoyed at the prospect of losing weight or seeing results. Starting a carnivore lifestyle will be difficult. You might be tired and exhausted. You should not rush into the diet or become overly enthusiastic about it. This can make you tired and make it difficult to stick to your plan.

The best thing you can do when starting this type of diet is to relax. If you're having a busy week or are under a lot of stress, you shouldn't start this diet right away. It's crucial to be able to unwind while on the diet, especially at the start.

If you can take a week off, this might be the best option. You can relax and nap without worrying about the work or activities you need to complete during this time. You may or may not be able to limit the amount of work you do during this time. Working remotely can be put off until the end of a big project, but it's not a good idea.

While this diet plan has many advantages and will make you feel great, the first week can be challenging. Your body will adjust to the new fuel source. Even if your favorite foods were healthy, you may have to give them up. You'll also have a lot more cravings for carbohydrates and sugars. You'll be grumpy and moody as a result of it all.

It's best not to put too much effort into these shifts in your emotions or feelings. It's easy to see why you'd be better off finishing a major project at work first, then waiting until things calm down, taking a break, and working from home to recover and adjust to your new diet plan.Poached Eggs

What's inside:

Eggs (2) Salt (.5 tsp.)

Butter (3 tbsp.) How to make:

1. To start this recipe, bring out a skillet and heat it up a bit.

Add in the butter and let it heat up for the next minute until soft.

2. At this time, gently crack the eggs, making sure that theyolks stay intact when you place them in the pan.

3. Sprinkle some salt over the eggs and then cook the eggsuntil they are all done to your liking.

4. Take the skillet off the heat, place the eggs on a plate, andenjoy. 5. 6.

Grilled Beef Patties

What's inside:

Aged Swiss cheese (8 slices) Salt (.5 tsp.)

Melted lard (1 tbsp.) Ground beef (2 lbs.)

For the fried eggs Free range eggs (8) Butter (2 Tbsp.) How to make:

1. To start this recipe, combine together the salt, meltedlard, and ground beef, mixing together lightly.

2. Once those are done, you can take the meat and shape itinto eight patties that are pretty even.

3. Turn on the grill and get it hot. Once it is warmed up, addthe eight patties to the grill and let them cook.

4. You will want the internal temperature of the meat to bearound 160 degrees. This can take grilling about seven minutes on each side.

5. Now you can work on the eggs. You can bring out twolarge skillets. Take a tablespoon of the butter and melt it on each one while heating them on the grill.

6. Break four eggs into a saucer and then gently slide theminto your pans. Reduce the heat to low. Try to place the eggs with the sunny side up and then cover the pan.

7. These need to cook for four minutes so that the yolksstart to thicken, but they don't get hard. If you would like to work with basted eggs, smear a bit of extra butter over them as you continue to cook.

8. Flip the eggs around until all of the sides are cookedproperly. Place the Swiss cheese on top of each egg until they start to melt. Serve the eggs on top of the burger patties and enjoy.

Sliced Cold Beef

What's inside:

Melted butter or ghee (1 tbsp.) Salt Cross rib roast (2 lb.) How 1. Take the roast out of the fridge and let it sit for half

anhour to an hour to warm up a bit and to ensure nice and even cooking.

2. After this time has passed, you can turn on the oven andlet it heat up to 250 degrees.

3. While the oven is heating up, you can take the beef andseason it with some salt all over. Then pour the melted ghee or butter on top to coat the beef lightly.

4. Put the beef into a baking dish or a roasting pan. Placethe pan into the oven and give it time to heat up.

5. After 2 hours, take the meat out of the oven and check thetemperature. Once it reaches 130 degrees, the meat will be medium rare. Cook for a bit longer if you want a different level of doneness.

6. Allow the beef to cool down on the counter for half anhour. Add to the fridge to cool down completely before slicing and serving.

Sous Vide Recipe

What's inside:

Ghee (1.5 tbsp.) Salt

Eye of the round roast (3 lbs.) How to make:

1. Take out a sous vide and fill it with some water. Set it toreach 140 degrees.

2. Bring out a FoodSaver bag and place the roast insidealong with a tablespoon of ghee. Vacuum seal the bag and place it in the fridge until the sous vide is warmed up

3. Once your sous vide reaches the right temperature, youcan place the vacuum-sealed beef inside and let it cook for some time.

4. After 24 hours, take the meat out of the bag and pat it dryusing some paper towels.

5. Take the rest of the ghee and heat it on a skillet. Seasonthe eye of the round with some salt and place it into the warmed up skillet.

6. Sear the meat on all sides for about 60 seconds each side.

Take the meat out of the skillet and let it rest before slicing up and serving.

Baked Eggs with Cream

What's inside:

Salt Eggs (2) Heavy whipping cream (2 tbsp.) Softened butter (.5 tbsp.) How to make:

1. Heat up the oven and give it some time to reach 425 degrees. While the oven is heating up, take out a four-ounce ramekin and coat it all over with some butter.

2. Add the cream into the ramekin and then crack the eggsinto it as well. Add this to the oven to bake.

3. After about 10 minutes, the whites of the eggs should bedone. Take the eggs out and then serve warm.

4. 5.

Bacon and Chorizo Sausage Bake

What's inside:

Bacon, cooked (3 slices) Salt Eggs (2) Chorizo sausage (4 oz.) Butter (1 tsp.) Lard or tallow (2 tbsp.) How 1. Turn on the oven and give it some time to heat up to

350 degrees. While the oven is heating up, use the butter to prepare two ramekins for this recipe.

2. Take out a skillet and heat up your lard or your tallowinside. This needs to heat up for three minutes to make soft.

3. Chop up the chorizo sausage in the pan until it is done.

When the sausage is done, divide it into equal amounts in each of the ramekins.

4. Slowly crack your egg into each ramekin and then seasonwith some salt. Place into the oven to bake.

5. After 13 minutes, the dish should be done. Take it out ofthe oven before topping with the bacon and serving.

Breakfast Meatloaf

What's inside:

Beef, ground (.5 lb.) Salt

Lard

Bacon strips (4) Parmesan cheese (1 c.) Egg (1) Butter (3 tbsp.)

Ground pork (.5 lb.) How to make:

1. To start this recipe, turn on the oven and let it heat up to350 degrees.

2. While the oven is warming up, take out a bowl and mixtogether salt, parmesan cheese, egg, beef, and ground pork. Make sure that the mixture sticks together.

3. Use this mixture to form two small logs and thenindividually tie them up with bacon strips starting from the top. Use as many bacon strips as you need for this.

4. Add the butter to a pan and then turn the heat on a highsetting. When the butter is melted, you can place the meatloaf in, allowing the bacon seam to face down to avoid spillage.

5. Flip and cook the meat on both sides to make it browned.

After the meat is browned, add the meat to a pan and place into the oven.

6. After 15 minutes of cooking, take the meatloaf out andallow it to rest a bit. Slice this up and serve warm.

Chicken Liver Pate What's inside:

Butter (.5 c.) Chicken liver (.5 lb.) Rosemary sprig Pepper Salt

Double cream (2 tbsp.) How to make:

1. Bring out a frying pan and melt a tablespoon of butterinside. When the butter is nice and melted, you can add in the chopped liver and let it cook for eight minutes.

2. After this time, you can add the liver into the foodprocessor. Add the leftover butter from the pan and some cheese as well.

3. Melt the rosemary, salt, pepper, thyme, and two moretablespoons of the butter together. When those are smooth, add them into the food processor with the liver.

4. Blend the liver in the food processor at this time until it issmooth. Pour the mixture into some ramekins.

5. Melt the rest of the butter that you have on the stove.

Then cover the pate with it and add some rosemary leaves on top.

6. Make sure to add this to the fridge to chill a bit beforeserving.

Lunches to Keep the Hunger Away

The next thing that we need to take a look at is the tasty lunches that can make or break your day. In the middle of the day, after working or playing hard so far today, you will want to make sure that you can have something that is tasty and easy to make. No one has the time to work on a meal that will take over an hour or more to make, but you want to make sure that you get to enjoy something that is tasty and healthy for you. Some of the tasty meals that you can enjoy on your lunch break, even on a leisurely weekend and are carnivore-friendly include:

Fried Chicken Hearts

What's inside:

Chicken hearts, quartered (500 g.) Butter (2 tbsp.) Fish sauce or salt to taste

How to make:

1. Take out a frying pan and heat up some of the butterinside until it has time to melt.

2. Once the butter melts, you can add in the chicken hearts.

Stirring them around the whole time, cook these until they brown. Then cover the frying pan.

3. Reduce the heat to a low setting now and let the chickenhearts cook until the pink center is gone. This can take around 15 minutes to be done.

4. Add in some of the fish sauce or some salt and then coverthe pan again. Cook for an additional five minutes before serving hot.

Baked Chicken Thighs

What's inside: Chicken thighs (4) How to make:

1. To start this recipe, turn on the oven and give it time toheat up to 400 degrees.

2. Bring out a baking dish or a baking pan and add thechicken thighs to it. Season these chicken thighs with some salt before placing into the preheated oven.

3. Allow these to bake for a bit. This is going to take about30 minutes to bake or go until the pink coloration that is in the bones starts to run clear.

4. After this time, take the pan out of the oven and servehot. 5. 6.

BBQ Trout

What's inside: Salt

Wild sea trout (6 lbs.) How to make:

1. To start this recipe, scale the wild trout, take the gills,eyes, and guts out and then wash it off. Pat dry with a kitchen towel all over to make sure that there are no running drips.

2. Take the fish and make some diagonal cuts on the sides.

Sprinkle a bit of salt into these cuts.

3. Bring out some newspapers and wrap the trout up inmultiple layers to ensure that it is sealed right. Use butchers string to help secure the newspapers.

4. Submerge the trout in the papers in cold water. This ismeant to help get the newspaper wet a little bit.

5. Turn on the grill and let it heat up. Add the fish into itand cook for about forty minutes. You can occasionally flip this around until it is ready.

6. After this time, you can take the fish off the grill andallow it time to cool down for a few minutes.

7. Cut off the string and remove the newspaper that wasaround the fish. Place the fish on a tray and flake off the fish with a fork. Enjoy the fish right away.

Smoked Lamb Ribs

What's inside:

Butter (1 tbsp.) Lamb rib chops (8) Pepper Salt (1 Tbsp.) How to make:

1. Take out the lamb chops and rub pepper and salt all over it to start this recipe.

2. Turn on the smoker and get it set up for indirect heating.

When you are ready, you can add the ribs onto the cooler part of the smoker so that they don't come in direct contact with the fire.

3. Cover the smoker and let these go for a bit. After an hour, take the ribs out and wrap them up with some foil.

4. Place them back into the smoker, letting the meat side be down, and continue to cook for another bit.

5. After another 35 minutes, you can flip these around and cook for another half an hour to finish.

6. Once this time is up, take the ribs from the smoker and give them half an hour to cool down.

7. Unwrap the ribs at this point and then serve.

Skinny Steaks

What's inside: Sliced beef sirloin (2 lbs.) Pepper

How to make:

1. Take your fatty beef strip and season it with the pepperand salt. Then place it in the fridge to set with the seasonings for the next two hours or so.

2. After this time is up, take the steak out of the fridge andpat it dry with the help of some paper towels.

3. Turn on the grill as high as you can get it, but leave thelid open. If you are using a charcoal grill, make sure that the coals are high enough to do this. If you are using a gas grill, lower the grate so that it is closer to your burner for this meal.

4. Add the meat to the hottest part of the grill. Flip it aroundto cool the hot surfaces, reduce the heat build-up, and to prevent the inside of the meat from overcooking.

5. You want to get the inside of the meat to 130 degrees,with a middle uniform and dark exterior with no grill marks.

6. Once it reaches the right internal temperature, you cantake the steak off the grill and enjoy.

Salami Crisps

What's inside: Salami slices (12) How to do it:

1. 325 degrees.

2. sheetand place a piece of parchment paper on the sheet.

3. Arrange the slices of salami out on the baking sheet,making sure that they are in one single layer. Add this to the oven and let it bake.

4. After about ten minutes, the edges of the salami shouldstart to curl up a bit. Remove them from the oven and set aside to cool for a few minutes before serving.

5. 6. Preheat the oven to 350°F. Remove a baking sheet from the oven as it heats up.

Salmon Slow-Baked

Inside the box:

Salmon fillets in their entirety Salt

butter (or ghee) that has been melted 1. Remove the salmon from the refrigerator and set it aside for a few minutes. We'll leave it out for about a half-hour to bring it closer to room temperature.

2. After half an hour, turn on the oven and allow it to heat to 275 degrees.

3. Remove the salmon from the pan and season with salt.

Place the salmon on a baking sheet with the butter or ghee spread all over it.

4. Heat the salmon in the oven for a few minutes. Check the salmon temperature after 30 minutes.

5. Remove the salmon from the oven and serve warm if the temperature reaches 120 degrees.

Flank Steak on the Broil

Inside the box:

Ghee, melted Sodium Steak on the side Making Instructions:

1. Remove the steak from the pan and set it aside to cool.

The chill from the fridge should have dissipated after 45 minutes, and you can begin the recipe. This period is crucial because it ensures even cooking.

2. Position the rack near the top of your oven so that the steak is only a few inches from the broiler when you place it inside.

3. Preheat the oven to broil and allow it to warm up for a few minutes.

4. Get a baking tray and place a wire cooling rack on top of it while the oven is heating up. Season the steak with salt and pepper, then pour the ghee over it evenly.

5. Place the prepared steak on the baking tray's cooling rack and bake it.

6. Remove the steak from the oven and broil it for a few minutes. After four minutes, flip the steak and broil for a few minutes more.

7. Check the internal temperature of the steak after another 6 minutes. It should be at least 125 degrees.

8. Remove the steak from the oven after it has reached the desired internal temperature and allow it to cool for five minutes. After that, serve the steak in strips.

Roasted Beef Chuck

Inside the box:

Parmesan cheese (shredded) Water vs. bone broth Salt

a bone-in chuck roast Making Instructions:

1. Remove the roast from the fridge and set it on the counter for about 60 minutes to help it loosen up and cook more evenly.

2. When the timer goes off, preheat the oven to 200 degrees. Season the roast with salt and pepper after cutting it into quarters. Place the seasoned beef and broth in a pot.

3. When placing the Dutch oven in the oven, do not put the lid on top of it. Cook until the broth and meat have reached a temperature of 120°F.

4. Cover the pot and turn the oven up to 250 degrees after two hours.

5. Cook for an additional three to four hours on this dish. You can check the meat for tenderness after that time has passed. If it requires a little more time, repeat the process at twenty to thirty minute intervals.

6. Remove the meat from the oven and set it aside to cool.

7. If desired, sprinkle some Parmesan on top of each individual serving before serving.

Bone Broth-Roasted Beef

Inside the box:

Bone broth or water. Salt

Roasting of chuck Making Instructions:

1. Remove the roast from the refrigerator and allow it to warm up for 60 minutes or so. This aids in the removal of the chill from the meat and ensures that it cooks evenly.

2. When the timer goes off, quarter the chuck roast and season it well.

3. Remove the bone broth from the Instant Pot and pour it into the bottom. The beef should be added last, followed by a tight seal on the lid.

4. Cook for 55 minutes on high pressure.

After that period of time has passed, you can relieve the pressure using the natural release method.

5. Remove the beef from the pot and shred it before serving once all of the pressure has been released.

Steak with an Inverted Sear

Inside the box:

Searing Sea Salt Steaks with animal fat

Making Instructions:

1. Remove the steak from the pan and set it on the counter to cool for about 45 minutes.

2. Sprinkle a pinch of salt on the steak. Remove the baking pan from the oven and place a wire cooling rack inside. Place the steak on top of this once it's all organized.

3. Preheat the oven to 275 degrees Fahrenheit, then turn it off. When the oven has reached the desired temperature, place the steak inside to bake.

4. Remove the steak from the oven after it has been cooking for 40 minutes. Heat a small amount of animal fat, such as bacon fat or ghee, in a large skillet over high heat.

5. Once those are warm, add the steak and cook it for a minute on each side, or until it reaches the desired temperature.

Steak with a T-bone cut that's been grilled

Inside the box:

Sodium

steaks with the t-bone

The snag is

the seeds of coriander pepper, cayenne Powdered garlic powdered onions Making Instructions:

1. Combine all of the dry spices in a small mixing bowl, grinding them together if necessary.

2. Remove the steaks from the pan and liberally salt them.

3. Marinate and chill the steaks for one to four hours in the fridge.

4. Preheat the grill after this time has passed, and then place the steaks on it to cook. To ensure that both sides are cooked, flip the steaks every two minutes.

5. Check the temperature of the meat after a few flips. It should be around 125 degrees inside if you want it medium rare. Cook until the chicken is cooked to your liking.

Family Dinners for the Caveman

Now it's time to get down to business! Supper is a great way for your family to get together and spend time together. It's nice to come home to a great meal that tastes good and is good and healthy for us after a long day at work and school and all of the other activities that we have to complete during the day. Thanks to the carnivore diet, the recipes below will help you get your meal on the table quickly while also allowing you to lose weight and improve your health.

Pulled Pork in the Crock-Pot

Inside the box:

Celtic salt is a type of salt that comes from the Mediterranean

Soup with chicken Rendering pork shoulder Making Instructions:

1. Get your slow cooker out and set it up to begin this recipe. Place the pork roast on the bottom when it's done.

2. Cover the slow cooker and pour the broth, salt, and butter all over the pork roast.

3. Reduce the heat to low and cook for 30 minutes. You can shut off the slow cooker after seven hours.

4. Remove the pork roast from the slow cooker and set aside to cool.

5. Shred the pork with your hands or a fork, then return it to the slow cooker shredded.

6. Toss the shredded meat in the juices to coat it, and serve immediately.

Pork Rind with Chicken

Inside the box:

Butter, salt

Pork rinds (ground) (2) Eggs breasts of chicken Making Instructions:

1. Season the chicken with salt after it has been removed from the oven. To make your batter, crack the eggs and whisk them in a separate bowl.

2. Place the pork crumbs on a plate and spread thinly.

3. When ready, dip the prepared chicken into the beaten egg first. Shake it a little to get rid of any excess liquid, then coat the chicken in bread crumbs.

4. Cook the chicken in the oven or in a pan.

Spread out the butter and bake some more after that.

5. The meal is ready to be served once the chicken has turned golden brown in color.

Shredded Chicken with Bacon

Inside the box:

(1) peppered slow-cooked chicken breast

Sodium

slices of diced bacon Making Instructions:

1. Get the slow cooker out of the cupboard and ready to go. Cook on a low setting with the chicken inside.

2. Shred the chicken using your hands or a fork after five hours in the slow cooker.

3. Heat up some butter in a skillet. Pan fry the bacon when the butter has melted.

4. When the bacon begins to render fat, add the shredded chicken and cook for a few minutes more.

5. Season with pepper and salt to taste after five minutes, and then serve.

Steaks in the South

Inside the box:

Sodium

Sirloin steaks that have been chopped h2o

Soup with beef

chili flakes Making Instructions:

1. To begin, remove the steak pieces and season them with salt and pepper.

2. Remove the butter from the freezer and place it in a large skillet or pan. You can add the steaks and cook them for a few minutes after the butter has melted.

3. Cook the steaks on each side until they begin to brown. Remove the steaks from the pan and place them in your slow cooker, which has been preheated.

4. Pour three cups of water and the broth into the skillet. Bring these liquids to a boil, then reduce the heat to medium high.

5. Put the mixture in the slow cooker once it has reached a boil.

Set the cooker to a low setting and cover it.

6. Remove the meat from the slow cooker and set it aside to serve after eight hours.

Bone Broth with Roasted Cream Chicken

Inside the box:

whipped cream (heavy) (2 c.) Salt

chicken breasts, whole Ghee is a type of butter that is made from Making
Instructions:

1. Remove the chicken from the refrigerator and place it on the counter to rest
for a while. Allow for a warm-up time of about an hour.

2. After this time has passed, turn on the oven and set it to 325 degrees
Fahrenheit. Take the whipping cream out of the fridge and warm it up a little
while the oven is heating up.

3. Remove the chicken from the pan and pat dry with paper towels. Salt the
inside and outside of the chicken generously.

4. Remove your Dutch oven from the oven and place it on the stove to begin
heating up. Before you add the chicken, add a little ghee to the pan.

5. In a Dutch oven, brown the chicken on both sides for about five minutes.
Add the whipping cream to the Dutch oven once the chicken has finished
browning.

6. Cover the Dutch oven and bake it. Check the temperature of the chicken after
60 minutes.

7. After you remove the chicken from the oven, let it rest for a few minutes
before carving. The chicken should be served with a dollop of cream on top.

Duck Breasts in a Pan

Salt is contained within the container.

Duck breasts, deboned Making Instructions:

1. Remove the duck breast from the refrigerator and allow it to come to room temperature before cooking. It could take up to an hour to complete this task.

2. Cut a crisscross pattern.in the fat and skin with a sharp knife, being careful not to cut too deeply into the meat. on all sides, season with salt

3. Heat the oven to 350 degrees Fahrenheit by turning it on. Heat a skillet that can be used in the oven. When the skillet is hot, place the duck breast skin-side down in it.

4. Allow for a ten-minute cooking time. If you notice that your skin is becoming too hot, lower the heat a little.

5. Once all of the sides have been seared, place the skin side down in the oven for a few minutes.

6. Cook the duck until it reaches a temperature of at least 165 degrees after another five to six minutes.

7. Remove the duck from the oven when it has reached this temperature and set aside to cool before slicing and serving.

Stove-Baked Pork Tenderloin

Salt is contained within the container.

Pork tenderloin is a type of pork tenderloin that is cooked Making Instructions:

1. Preheat the oven to 350 degrees Fahrenheit, then turn it off. Remove any silver skin from the tenderloin with the help of a boning knife. After that, the pork can be cut into medallions or left whole.

2. Sprinkle salt on all sides of the pork. Remove an oven-safe skillet from the stove and heat it up. Ghee or bacon fat can be added to the mix.

3. Cook the porkinside in the bacon fat or ghee that has warmed up. For about a minute, cook this on all sides.

4. Now you can transfer the pork to the oven and finish cooking it. It'll take you about ten minutes to finish this.

5. Allow ten minutes for the pork to rest before slicing and serving.

Turkey Roasting

Inside the box:

ghee (ghee) that has been softened Salt

Neck and giblets have been removed from a turkey. Making Instructions:

1. Remove the turkey from the refrigerator and set it out to rest for 30 minutes on the counter. Take some time to deconstruct it after that.

2. Preheat oven to 450 degrees Fahrenheit. To prepare your oven, place the rack in the lower third.

3. Dry the turkey and gently pull the skin away from the meat, but not completely.

4. Slather as much butter or ghee as you can between the meat and the skin, then replace the skin. Salt and pepper the entire turkey.

5. Place the turkey parts in the roasting pan and bake. Reduce the oven's temperature to 325 degrees after 25 minutes. Allow the turkey to absorb all of its juices for a few moments.

6. Check the turkey's temperature again after another 30 minutes. The breasts should be 145 degrees, while the thighs and legs should be 165 degrees.

7. Once the turkey has reached the right temperature, take itout of the oven and give it ten to fifteen minutes to cool down.

Serve warm.

Slow Cooker Beef Tongue

Inside the box:

Bone broth or water. Salt

Rinsed beef tongue (4 lbs) (4 lbs.) Making Instructions:

1. Rinse the beef tongue off. Lay it out flat and then seasonwith some salt before adding to your prepared slow cooker.

2. Make sure to add enough of the water or the broth tocover the tongue up, and then place the lid on top of the slow cooker.

3. Turn the slow cooker on to the low setting to cook. Afterten hours, turn the slow cooker off. Carefully remove the hot tongue and pull the skin off gently. At this point, it should come off pretty easily.

4. Now, slice up the beef and sear it in a skillet with somehot butter. You can also choose to shred the beef with the help of two forks.

5. Season with more salt if needed before serving. Keep theleftover liquid to use as a stock.

Oyster Cream Panfry

Inside the box:

Salt

Heavy cream (.5 c.) Bone broth (.25 c.) Ghee or butter (1 tsp.)

Shucked fresh oysters (12) Making Instructions:

1. To start this recipe, add the oysters to a small pan. Heatup some of the butter or ghee on medium heat and start cooking.

2. Pour the broth on top. When it begins to simmer andfroth, gently stir the oysters until their edges begin to turn.

3. After this time, add in the cream and bring it to a simmer.

Season the whole thing with some salt and take the pan off the heat.

4. Allow your oysters to sit in the sauce for a few minutes towarm up and soak in the sauce. Transfer this dish to some bowls and then serve.

Steamed Clams or Mussels

Inside the box:

Mussels (1 lb. per person) Bone broth (.5 c.)

Ghee is a type of butter that is made from Making Instructions:

1. Take out a big pot that has a lid. Add in the ghee or somebutter and let it melt on medium heat.

2. After the butter has some time to melt, add in the bonebroth and the mussels to the pot. Add the lid to the top.

3. Turn the heat of the stove to high setting and cook thesefor a bit. After three minutes, shake the pot a bit, making sure that the lid is still on, and rotate the mussels.

4. Let these cook for a bit longer. After another 5 minutes,you can take the pot off the heat. Take the mussels out of the pot and place into a serving bowl.

5. Ladle the broth over the mussels, but make sure to leavethe sediment that is there at the bottom of the pot and enjoy.

Chicken Livers Wrapped with Bacon

Inside the box:

Ghee or butter (3 oz.) Bacon, cut in half (.5 lbs.) Chicken livers (1 lb.) How to make: 1. Take the butter and place it into a pan to heat up

andbecome melted.

2. Once the butter or ghee is melted, you can add in thechicken livers and let it brown on both sides before taking them out of the heat.

3. Take a half strip of bacon and wrap it around each of thepieces of chicken livers. Secure the bacon in place with some toothpicks.

4. Add these back into the skillet and pan fry the livers andthe bacon until the bacon has become nice and crisp. 5. Once this happens, take the chicken livers

and bacon outof the skillet, take the toothpicks out of the meats, and then serve this warm.

Slow Cooker Chicken Gizzards

Inside the box:

Pepper Salt Beef broth (8 c.) Chicken hearts (1 bag)

Chicken gizzards (1 bag) Making Instructions:

1. To start this recipe, you can take the chicken parts andrinse them with some water.

2. Set up the slow cooker and then add the gizzards insidefirst. Then add in the chicken hearts and add the pepper and salt.

3. Cover the gizzards and the heart with some of the beefbroth and then add the lid onto the slow cooker.

4. Put the slow cooker on a heat setting that is low. Aftereight hours, the chicken parts will be done and you can serve warm.

Conclusion

Thank you for making it through to the end of Carnivore Diet. Let's hope it was informative and able to provide you with all of the tools you need to achieve your goals whatever they may be.

The next step is to get started on the carnivore diet and see if it is the right choice for you. There are a lot of different diet plans out there and many times, they end up contradicting each other and confusing the person who is trying to go on them. Some of them may work but are too hard to maintain for a long period of time, and others may be easier, but they just don't work at all.

This can leave the dieter feeling like a failure, and they wonder if they can ever lose the weight and feel good again.

The carnivore diet is going to be a bit different than this. Instead of making up a bunch of complicated rules that are hard to follow, the carnivore diet is going to instead focus on keeping things simple and taking us back to our roots. On this diet plan, you will focus on just eating animal products. This means lots of meat, including fish, eggs, butter, and some aged cheese.

Outside of that, the other foods need to be avoided.

Those who follow this kind of diet plan are going to see some great results. You will find that there are a few weeks of transitioning away from the traditional foods that you like to enjoy, including the carbs, sugars, and even produce. But once the body adjusts and you see some of the great meals that you are able to enjoy on this plan, you will be wondering why you didn't try this out before!

This guidebook took some time to talk about the carnivore diet and all of the steps that you can take to see some results with it. There is so much to love when it comes to this diet plan, and if you are able to get on it and maintain it, you are sure to see the results.

Inside this guidebook, we have given you the steps that you need to see some great results. We talked about the basics of this diet plan, the foods that you are allowed to consume, the way that exercise can fit into the plan, and so much more. You even get the benefit of seeing some delicious meals and a full meal plan that can make this diet plan the best option for you.

If you are tired of dieting and getting confused by all of the rules and recommendations that come with other diet plans, and you want a plan that actually works and is simple to keep up with, the carnivore diet might be the best one for you.

CPSIA information can be obtained
at www.ICGtesting.com
Printed in the USA
BVHW050227260122
627128BV00007B/523